CANDLES IN BABYLON

Books by Denise Levertov

Poetry

The Double Image

Here and Now

Overland to the Islands

With Eyes at the Back of Our Heads

The Jacob's Ladder

O Taste and See

The Sorrow Dance

Relearning the Alphabet

To Stay Alive

Footprints

The Freeing of the Dust

Life in the Forest

Collected Earlier Poems 1940–1960

Prose

The Poet in the World

Light Up the Cave

Translations

Guillevic/Selected Poems

Denise Levertov

Candles in Babylon

A New Directions Book

ACKNOWLEDGMENTS
Grateful acknowledgment is given to the magazines and journals in which some of these poems first appeared: *Alliance for Survival, The Ark, Chicago Review, Harvard Magazine, Imprint, In These Times, Intrepid* (Bill Williams and Flossie Special), *Jawbone Press, Lost Glove, Nantucket Review, New Letters, Paris Review, Peak Load Newsletter, Poetry East, Polis Magazine, Seer, Southern Poetry Review, Tendril, Texas Arts Journal, Two Pears Press, Willow Springs Magazine,* and *WIN Magazine.*

"Mass for the Day of St. Thomas Didymus" first appeared in a limited edition from William B. Ewert, Publisher; "Talking in the Dark" was originally published as a Square Zero Editions broadside.

The sequence *Pig Dreams* was first published in 1981 in a separate edition by Countryman Press with illustrations by Libe Coolidge.

Manufactured in the United States of America
First published clothbound and as
New Directions Paperbook 533 in 1982
Published simultaneously in Canada by George J. McLeod, Ltd., Toronto

Library of Congress Cataloging in Publication Data
Levertov, Denise, 1923–
    Candles in Babylon.
    (A New Directions Book)
    Includes bibliographical references.
    I. Title.
ps3562.e8876c3   1982   811'.54   81-22289
isbn 0-8112-0830-3   aacr2
isbn 0-8112-0831-1 (pbk.)

New Directions Books are published for James Laughlin
by New Directions Publishing Corporation
80 Eighth Avenue, New York 10011

Contents

Candles in Babylon

Through the midnight streets of Babylon
between the steel towers of their arsenals,
between the torture castles with no windows,
we race by barefoot, holding tight
our candles, trying to shield
the shivering flames, crying
'Sleepers Awake!'
                hoping
the rhyme's promise was true,
that we may return
from this place of terror
home to a calm dawn and
the work we had just begun.

I
WANDERER'S DAYSONG

Dwellers at the Hermitage

Grief sinks and sinks
into the old mineshaft
under their house,
how deep, who knows.
When they have need
for it, it's there.

Their joys
refused to share themselves,
fed from the hand
of one alone, browsed
for days in dappled
pathless woods
untamed.

Sorrow
is what one shares,
they say;
and happiness, the wistful gold
of our solitudes, is what
our dearest lovers,
our wingéd friends,
leave with us, in trust.

My daughters, the old woman says, the weaver
                    of fictions, tapestries
                    from which she pulls
                    only a single thread each day, pursuing
                    the theme at night—
my daughters? Delicate bloom
of polished stone. Their hair
ripples and shines like water, and mine
is dry and crisp as moss in fall.

Trunk, limbs, bark; roots under all of it:
the tree I am, she says, blossoms year after year,
random, euphoric;
the bees are young, who nuzzle their fur
into my many fragile hearts.
My daughters
have yet to bear
their fruit,
they have not imagined
the weight of it.

Mother and Father have fulfilled their promise:
      the overture, the rise of the curtain, the imagined pomp
      of magic and artifice, all
      glows, as if music
      were made of candle flames, all
      flows, as if dancers
      were golden oil of music,
      the theater's marvelous smell is also
      the prickle of crimson velvet on bare skin—but
            at the marrow of all this joy, the child
            is swept by a sudden
            chill of patience: notices wearily
            the abyss that Time
            opens before it.
                        Careful, careful—
      no one must share
      this knowledge.
The child tenderly, tense with protective love,
guards their innocent happiness,
      kind Father,
      kind Mother.
                        Quickly! Back to the long-desired,
the even-better-than-hoped-for treat.
            Has one not run
            more than once
         back from a strip of woods to open sunlight,
         hastily laughing, uttering
         not a word about
                 white
                    bones
      strewn in ivy,
            and old feathers, raggéd?

I send my messages ahead of me.
You read them, they speak to you
in siren tongues, ears of flame
spring from your heads to take them.

When I arrive, you love me,
for I sing those messages you've
learned by heart, and bring,
as housegifts, new ones. You hear

yourselves in them,
self after self. Your solitudes
utter their runes, your own
voices begin to rise in your throats.

But soon you love me less.
I brought with me
too much, too many laden coffers,
the panoply of residence,

improper to a visit.
Silks and furs, my enormous wings,
my crutches, and my spare crutches,
my desire to please, and worse—

my desire to judge what is right.

I take up
so much space.
You are living on what you can find,
you don't want charity, and you can't
support lingering guests.

When I leave, I leave
alone, as I came.

One by one
they fall away—

all whom they really
wanted to keep. People.
Things that were more than things.

The dog, the cat,
the doll with a silk dress,
the red penknife:
those were the first to go.

Then father, mother,
sister, brother,
wife and husband.
Now the child.

The child is grown,
the child is gone,
the child has said,
Don't touch me, don't call me,

your lights have gone out,
I don't love you.
No more.

The distant child
casts a tall shadow:
that's the dark.
And they are small.

The world is brittle,
seamed with cracks,
ready to shatter. Now

7

the old man steps
into a boat,
rows down the rainy street.
Old woman, she climbs up

into the steeple's eye.
Transmogrified, she's
the clapper of the bell.

The tolling begins.

Try to remember, every April, not this one only
you feel you are walking underwater
in a lake stained by your blood.

When the east wind rips the sunlight
your neck feels thin and weak, your clothes
don't warm you.

You feel you are lurching away from
deft shears, rough hands, your fleece
lies at the shepherd's feet.

And in the first warm days each step
pushes you against a weight,
and you don't want

to resist that weight,
you want to stop, to return
to darkness
          —but treaties made
over your head force you to
waver forward.

Yes, this year you feel
at a loss, there is no Demeter
to whom to return

if for a moment you saw
yourself as Persephone.
It is she, Demeter, has gone
        down to the dark.

Or if it is Orpheus drawing you forth,
Eurydice,
he is inexorable, and does not look back

to let you go.

You are appalled to consider you may be destined
to live to a hundred.
But it is April,

there is nothing unique in your losses,
your pain is commonplace
and your road ordained:

your steps will hurt you,
you will arrive
as usual

at some condition you name *summer:*

> an ample landscape,
> voluptuous, calm,
> of large, very still trees,
> water meadows, dreamy
> savannah distances,

where you will gather strength,
pulling ripe fruit from the boughs,
for winter and spring,
forgotten seasons.

Try to remember it is always this way.
You live
this April's pain
now,

you will come
to other Aprils,
each will astonish you.

People like me can't feel
the full rush of air around us as we
plunge into swansdown billows of
dustgold fathomless happenstance—

                  we leap but
we've known the leaden no-light
that's not darkness, that is
eclipse. When green
loses its green spirit. When vertigo
takes the wheeling swifts and drops them like separate
pebbles of rain. When rain
begins and stops, appalled at the discourse of bones it makes
on cracked clay. That no-light blunted us.

Yes, and we've known, we know
every day, our tall mothers and fathers
are gone, no one
has known us always,
we are ancient orphans,
parchment skins stretched upon crutches,
inscribed with epitaphs.

When mirrors tell us white beards
have not yet appeared from within us

nor pendulous breasts
hung themselves on our torsos like bundles
of parched herbs,

when the sun
gnaws its way out of its cage again,

when the skylark
tears itself out of our throats,

we do leap, we do
plunge into skylake's
haze of promise. But we feel

along with the air rushing, our own breath
rushing
out of us.
        See
for an instant the arc of
our vanishing.

The Dragonfly-Mother[*]

I was setting out from my house
to keep my promise

but the Dragonfly-Mother stopped me.

I was to speak to a multitude
for a good cause, but at home

the Dragonfly-Mother was listening
not to a speech but to the creak of
                          stretching tissue,
tense hum of leaves unfurling.

Who is the Dragonfly-Mother?
What does she do?

She is the one who hovers
on stairways of air,
                          sometimes almost
grazing your cheekbone,
she is the one who darts unforeseeably
into unsuspected dimensions,

who sees in water
her own blue fire zigzag, and lifts
her self in laughter
into the tearful pale sky

that sails blurred clouds in the stream.

•

She sat at my round table,

* See note on page 117.

we told one another dreams,
I stayed home breaking my promise.

When she left I slept
three hours, and arose

and wrote. I remember the cold
Waterwoman, in dragonfly dresses

and blue shoes, long ago.
She is the same,

whose children were thin,
left at home when she went out dancing.
She is the Dragonfly-Mother,

that cold
is only the rush of air

swiftness brings.
There is a summer
over the water, over

the river mirrors
where she hovers, a summer
fertile, abundant, where dreams
grow into acts and journeys.

Her children
are swimmers, nymphs and newts, metamorphic.
                    When she tells
her stories she listens; when she listens
she tells you the story you utter.

                              •

When I broke my promise,
and slept, and later

cooked and ate the food she had bought
and left in my kitchen,

I kept a tryst with myself,
a long promise that can be fulfilled
only poem by poem,
broken over and over.

> I too,
a creature, grow among reeds,
> in mud, in air,
in sunbright cold, in fever
of blue-gold zenith, winds
of passage.

> Dragonfly-Mother's
a messenger,
if I don't trust her
I can't keep faith.

> There is a summer
in the sleep
of broken promises, fertile dreams,
acts of passage, hovering
journeys over the fathomless waters.

There are times
>>no one seems to notice
>>>>when I move weightlessly
not flying exactly
>>but stepping as if in
>>>>>>7 league boots—
yet not
>>leagues at a time,
>>>>merely a modest matter of
feet or at most yards.
I don't
>>know how it is that
>>>>no one sees it, or
could it be they do, and don't
>>>>mention it
>>>>>>from embarrassment?
Certainly
>>it is strange, I know,
>>>>>>and yet
there's no need for anyone to
>>>>feel afraid. I prefer
not to suppose
>>envy could cause their silence.
>>>>>>**No,**
more likely it's only
>>>>so improbable,
>>>>>>they don't believe
their eyes.
For myself, I confess,
>>>>it is a
>>>>>>great delight—
the springiness,
>>>>the soft
>>>>>>swing of it.

Especially I like
　　　　　to traverse
　　　　　　　　　a landscape this way
when there is no one
　　　　　　looking.
There is
　　　　a low hill rising from marshland I've been to lately
　　　　　　　　　　　　　at twilight, an hour
of mist and mauve loomings of
　　　　　　　　　vast and benevolent
　　　　　　　　　　　　　ancient trees—
I returned
　　　only when sensing myself
　　　　　　　　too close to the deepening water.

17

On the way to the
valley of transformation
one arrives sometimes at
those evenings, late, the mirror gives one,
      (softlit, and folds or falls
      of silk or wool
      conspiring like the eyes of
      loyal friends)
when one's own image greets one with pleasure.
Pleasure! How one smiles back, still hearing
goodnights and laughter,
      how one turns up the radio's midnight blues
and dances,
and checks the mirror and sees,
yes, one is dancing there, looking
just the way dancers do when one watches
           wistfully from the outskirts of music.
On the way down there are
these way stations
         where goodbyes
are festive lanterns by the edge of a lake
and the face in the glass has shed its agelines as if
they were the mirage.

The Art of the Octopus: Variations on a Found Theme

The octopus is a solitary creature, and for it,
*   any shelter it can find is home.*
Connoisseur of continents,
it embraces gratefully the flatlands where shadows
dance the largesse of sky and transpose
the gestures of clouds whose wagon trains
roll across domed springtime,

while simultaneously
another caressive tentacle
strokes the steel girders of the mountains'
refusal to budge, admiring their steadfast ranks,
their doctrine of patience.

When it gave up its protective shell it developed
many skills and virtues.

It can, for example, curl itself small
to live in attics where daybreak
is an alertness of red rooftiles that a moment ago
were a vague brown at the western window,
or it can untwine, stretching out starbeams into voluptuous
unexplored chains of high-vaulted thronerooms
beyond the scan of hurried, bone-aching throngs
below in the long streets.
                         These are skills.
Virtues? Transparently
it ingests contrast, regarding it humbly
as joy. Nourished,
it gives forth peculiar light, a smoky radiance.
Some see this aura. Some think it poisonous,
others desire it. Of those who enter
that bright cloud, some vanish. Others begin
to grow long, wavering, extra arms, godlike,

so that at last they touch
many things at once, and reach
towards everything; they too begin
the solitary dance.

May mornings wear
light cashmere shawls of quietness,
brush back waterfalls of
burnished silk from
clear and round brows.
When we see them approaching
over lawns, trailing
dewdark shadows and footprints,
we remember, ah,
yes, the May mornings,
how could we have forgotten,
what solace it would have been
to think of them,
what solace
it would be in the bitter violence
of fire then ice again we
apprehend—but
it seems the May mornings
are a presence known
only as they pass
lightstepped, seriously smiling, bearing
each a leaflined basket
of wakening flowers.

Have you ever heard the rain at night
streaming its flaxen hair against
the walls of your house?

Have you ever heard the rain at night
drifting its black, shiny, seaweed hair
through multistoreyed arcades of leaves?

And have you risen then
from bed and felt your way
to the window, and raised the blind, and seen

> stillness, unmisted moonlight, the air
> dry? Street and garden
> empty and silent?

You had been lying awake; the rain
was no dream. Yet where is it?

When did that rain descend and descend,
filling your chalices
until their petals loosened

and wafted
down to rest
on grass and the wet ground,

and your roots in their burrows
stretched and sighed?

II
PIG DREAMS

The beginning: piglet among piglets,
the soft mud caking
our mother's teats.
Sweetsqueal, grunt:
her stiff white lashes, the sleepy
glint of her precious
tiny eyes.

                    ●

But I am Sylvia. Chosen.
I was established
pet. To be
the pig of dreams, the pig
any of us could be,
        taken out of the sty,
        away from the ravaged soil of pig-yards,
        freed from boredom and ugliness.
I was chosen to live without dread of slaughter.

                    ●

For three days, after they took me,
I hungered. Nowhere a teat to suck from,
no piglet siblings to jostle and nudge.
At last
        in the full moon's sacred light
        in the human room where I'd run
        in circles till my tapping trotters
        almost gave way,
the He-human
           naked and white as my
           lost mother,
bent on all-fours over my untouched bowl,
his beard a veil before me,

and with musical loud sounds of guzzling
showed me *eating*. Gave me
the joy of survival.

•

Quicklearner, soon
I could hold my shit.
I was rocked in warm
human arms.
I liked laps, the thighs
of humans.
Cuddling.
      Every pig
could be cuddled if there were justice.
      Every human
could have its intelligent pig,
      every pig
its dextrous human. Our lives
would be rich as creamy corn,
tasty as acorns.

Dogbrothers

Pigalone. Sylvia.
Sylvia Orphan Onlypig.
Even my She-human's lap
could not console.
But then I found
my Dogbrothers.
Bark and growl,
dog-laugh, waving
tails and the joy
of chasing, of whirling,
squealing, my dainty trotters

trilling beneath me
sharp and sure!
Of huddling to doze
in warm quickbreathing
muddle of dogs,
almost believing
I, Sylvia,
am dog not pig.

The Catpig

John the Cat
is most my brother,
almost pig

even though he
leaps among branches,
climbs to high shelves,
is silky.

Black and white Catpig,
I outgrew you,
but once we matched.

She-human gave us
our milk from
our pitcher.

Quiet we sat
under the sumacs of Vermont
and watched

the birds leave,
the first snow
pepper each other's
somber faces.

At the quick of winter
moonbrightest
snowdeepest

we would set out.
I'd run up my ramp
into the pickup,

we'd rattle and shake
two midnight miles
to the right hill.

Then on foot,
slither and struggle
up it—

they'd
ready their sled
and toboggan down

and I'd
put down my nose and
spread my ears and

tear down beside them,
fountains of snow
spurting around me:

I and my Humans
shouting, grunting,
the three of us

wild with joy,
just missing
the huge maples.

Yes, over and over
up to the top of the
diamond hill—

the leanest, the fastest,
most snow-and-moon-and-midnight-bewitched
pig in the world!

                                    The Bride

They sent me away to be bred.
I was afraid, going down the ramp
from the truck to the strange barn,
I tried to run for the farmyard—strangers
shouted, they drove me inside.

In the barn a beautiful, imperious boar
dwelt in majesty. They brought me to him.
In the hot smell of him, I who was delicate,
        Sylvia the pet,
                    who smelled of
        acorns and the windscoured pasture,
        I, Sylvia the Dreamer,
was brought low,
was brought
into the depths
of desire.
        I steeped my soul
                        in the sweet dirt,
                        the stench of
        My Lord Boar

                        •

Terrible, after the sensuous dark,
                the week of passion and feasting,

—terrible my return.
I screamed when they dragged me
outdoors to the truck. Harsh light
jumped at my eyes. My body's weight
sagged on my slender legs.

In the house of My Lord Boar
I had eaten rich swill.

Back home, I headed for my
private house, the house of Sylvia—
and my swill-swollen body
   would not enter,
   could not fit.

In shame I lay
many nights
on the ground outside my Humans' window
and passed my days silent and humble
in the bare pasture, until I was lean again,
    until I could enter
     my maiden chamber once more.

But now I carried in me
the fruit of my mating.

Her Task

My piglets cling to me,
perfect, quickbreathing, plump—
kernels of pearly sweetcorn,
milky with my milk.

These shall I housetrain, I swear it,
these shall dwell like their mother

among dextrous humans, to teach them
pig-wisdom. O Isis, bless
thy pig's piglets.

Her Secret

In the humans' house
fine things abound:
furniture, rugs by the hearth,
bowls and pitchers, freezer and fridge,
closets of food, baskets of apples,
the Musical Saw on which
my He-human plays
           the songs I dream . . .

In my neat A-frame
they think there is nothing,
only the clean straw of my bed.
But under the floor I gather
beautiful tins, nutshells, ribbons,
shining buttons, the thousand baubles
a pig desires.

They are well hidden.
Piglets shall find one day
an inheritance of shapes,
textures, mysterious substances—

Rubber! Velvet! Aluminum! Paper!

Yes, I am founding,
    stick by stick,
        wrapper by wrapper,
        trinkets, toys—
Civilization!

The dream is blood: I swim,
which is forbidden to pigs,
and the doom comes: my sharp
flailing feet cut
into my thick throat
and the river water
is stained, and fills, and
thickens with bright blood
and darkens, and I'm
choking, drained,
too weak to heave
out of the sticky
crimson mud, and
I sink and sink in it
screaming, and then
voiceless, and
when I wake it's
the dark of the moon.

Yet, when I was young,
not knowing the prohibition,
I did swim. The corn
was tall, and my skin
was dry as old
parchment of husks,
the creviced earth
scorched, and no rain
had fallen
for long and long:
when my She-human plunged
into the lovely
cool and wet river,
I too
plunged, and swam.
It was easy to me

as if the water
were air, and I
a young bird in flight.
My pig-wings
flailed, but my throat
was not slit, and we crossed
the river, and rested
under splashed leaves
on the far shore,
and I thought I would always
be Sylvia Waterpig.
O it was sweet
to be upborne
on the fresh-running current,
a challenge to push
across it and gain
the moss and shade.
I escaped
the doom
then.
    But I grew
heavier, thick in the throat,
properly pigshaped,
and learned the Law.
And now,
this dream, on some
black nights, fills up
my bowl of sleep
with terror,
with blood.

Her Lament

When they caressed
and held in loving arms
the small pig that I was,

I was so glad, I blessed
my singular fate.
How could I know
my Humans would not grow
to fit me, as I became
Sylvia the Sow?
He-and-She-Human stayed the same, and now
even look smaller.
Perhaps I should not have learned
to adore
pleasures that could not last?
I grew so fast.
My destiny
kept me lean, and yet
my weight increased.
Great Sylvia, I must stay
under the table at the humans' feast.
And once, scratching my back on it,
I made the table fall
dishes and all!
How could a cherished piglet
have grown so tall?

Her Sadness

When days are short,
mountains already
white-headed, the west
red in its branchy
leafless nest, I know

more than a simple
sow should know.

I know
the days of a pig—

and the days of dogbrothers, catpigs,
cud-chewing cowfriends—
are numbered,

even the days of
Sylvia the Pet,

even the days
of humans are numbered.
Already

laps are denied me,
I cannot be cuddled,
they scratch my ears
as if I were anypig, fattening for bacon.

I shall grow heavier still,
even though I walk
for miles with my Humans,
through field and forest.

Mortality
weighs on my shoulders,
I know
too much about Time for a pig.

Her Sister

Kaya, my gentle
              Jersey cowfriend,
                             you are no pig,
you are slow to think,
                your moods
                        are like rounded clouds

drifting over the pasture,
        casting
           pleasant shadows.
You lift your head
      slowly
        up from the grass
to greet me.
     Occupied
       with your cud, you are
all cow,
    yet we are friends,
        or even sisters.
We worship
    the same goddess,
       we look
to the same humans
    with love,
      for love.
When I tread
    the mud in pigpatterns
        after a shower,
my footprints shine
    and reflect the sky:
       in this
they resemble your huge
    kindly eyes.
       My own
are small,
   as befits a pig,
     but I behold your steep
graygold side,
   a bulwark
     beside me.

I, Sylvia, tell you, my piglets:
it has been given me
to spend a whole day up to my snout
in the velvet wetness that is mud:

and to walk undriven, at dusk,
back to the human-house
and be welcomed there:

welcomed by humans and cats and dogs,
not reproached for my mantle
of graying mud:

welcomed, and given to eat
a food of human magic, resembling mud
and tasting
of bliss: and its holy name
is *chocolate*.

I, Sylvia, your mother,
have known
the grace of pig-joy.

Her Judgement

I love my own Humans and their friends,
but let it be said,
that my litters may heed it well,
their race is dangerous.

They mock the race of Swine, and call
'swinish' men they condemn.

Have they not appetites? Do *we*
plan for slaughter to fill our troughs?

Their fat ones, despised, waddle large-footed,
· their thin ones hoard
inedible discs and scraps
called 'money.' Us they fatten,
us they exchange for this;

and they breed us not that our life
may be whole, pig-life
thriving alongside dog-life, bird-life,
grass-life, all
the lives of earth-creatures,

but that we may be devoured. Yet,
it's not being killed for food
destroys us. Other animals
hunt one another. But only Humans,

I think, first corrupt their prey
as we are corrupted, stuffed with temptation
until we can't move,

crowded until we turn on each other,
our name and nature abused.

It is their greed
overfattens us.
Dirt we lie in
is never unclean as their minds,
who take our deformed lives
without thought, without
respect for the Spirit Pig.

Pig-song

Walnut, hickory, beechmast,
apples and apples, a meadow
of applegrass dapple.
Walnut, hickory, beechmast.
And over the sunfall slope,
cool of the dark mudwallow.

Her Vision

My human love, my She-human,
speaks to me in Piggish. She knows
my thoughts, she sees my emotions
flower and fade, fade and flower
as my destiny unrolls
its carpet, its ice and apples.

Not even she
knows all my dreams.
Under the russet sky
at dusk
I have seen
the Great Boar pass

invisible save to me.

His tusks are
flecked with skyfoam.
His eyes
red stars.

O Isis my goddess,
my goddess Isis,
forget not thy pig.

Isis Speaks

Sylvia, my faithful
Petpig, teacher
of humans, fount
of pig-wisdom:
you shall yet know
the grief of parting:
your humans, bowed with regret,
shall leave you.
But hear me,
this is no dream:
the time shall come
when you shall dwell,
revered,
in a house of your own
even finer than that you have.
And though you no longer
enter the houses of humans,
in springtimes to come
your black hide shall be strewn
with constellations of blossom.
Yes, in the deep summers,
apples shall bounce on your roof,
the ripe and round
fruit of your own appletree.
There you shall live long, and at peace,
redreaming the lore of your destiny.

III
PEOPLE, PLACES, VISIONS

An Arrival (North Wales, 1897)

The orphan arrived in outlandish hat,
proud pain of new button boots.
Her moss-agate eyes
photographed views of the noonday sleepy town
no one had noticed. Nostrils flaring,
she sniffed odors of hay and stone,
                    absence of Glamorgan coaldust,
and pasted her observations quickly
into the huge album of her mind.
Cousins, ready to back off like heifers
were staring:
                    amazed, they received
the gold funeral sovereigns she dispensed
along with talk strange to them as a sailor's parrot.

Auntie confiscated the gold;
the mourning finery, agleam with jet,
was put by to be altered. It had been chosen
by the child herself and was thought
unsuitable. She was to be
the minister's niece, now,
not her father's daughter.
                    Alone,
she would cut her way through a new world's
graystone chapels, the steep and sideways
rockface cottages climbing
mountain streets,

enquiring, turning things over
in her heart,
                    weeping only in rage or when
the choirs in their great and dark and
golden glory broke forth and the hills
skipped like lambs.

i

From under wide wings of blackest velvet
—a hat such as the Duse might have worn—
peered out at me my mother,
tiny and silver-white, her ancient skin delicately
pink, her eyes their familiar very dark
pebble-green, flecked with amber. 'Mother,'
I cried or mumbled, urgent but even now
embarrassed, 'can you forgive me? Did you,
as I've feared and feared, feel betrayed
when I failed to be there
at the worst time, and returned
too late? Am I forgiven?' But she looked vague
under the velvet, the ostrich-down, her face small;
if she said mildly, 'There is nothing to forgive,'
it seemed likely she wasn't listening,
she was preoccupied with some concerns
of that other life, and when she faded
I was left unabsolved still, the raven drama
of her hat more vivid to me
than she in her polite inattention.
        This, I told myself,
is fitting: if the dead live
for a while in partial semblances
of their past selves, they have no time
to bear grudges or to bless us;
their own present
holds them intent. Yet perhaps
sometimes they dream us.

ii

Another time she arrived
through the French window at home
(the house that has no place now
to *be* in, except in me)
with gypsy bundles, laughing, excited,
old but not ancient yet, strong,
a lone traveller.
                    It was clear
she had come only to visit,
not to remain—
'It was a long trip,' she said,
'from Heaven to here!'
and we hugged and laughed and were comfortable.
I saw each thread
in the tapestry seat of a forgotten chair,
cloudy figures in the marble mantelpiece,
each detail of that vanished room.
A joyful meeting, and she
incandescent with joy.
Yet next day my perplexed grief
did not lift away but still,
like a mallard with clipped wings
circles me summer and winter, settled
for life in my life's reedy lake.

A Saxon peasant girl
darning a sock, is telling
household tales to her sleepy daughters.
'So the roasting pan
said to the little brown hen—'
Looking up, she sees
their eyes have closed. No need
to tell what it said.
She trims the lamp,
sits in the small circle of gold;
dark of the room's corners
is in league with the dark outside.
The forest
is not the familiar forest of proper trees
whose names she knew,
woodland of midsummer Sunday walks,
Grandmother's märchen,
understandable dangers.
This is the jungle. Here
enormous dazzling butterflies lure her children
into the underbrush among the snakes.
Birds whose violent beauty
makes her long for the humble brown
of a thrush, scream through vines
that everywhere
hide those unknowable trees, trunks
masked in green and blossom, boughs
a ceiling of dense foliage and flashes
of hot sky. At times
a band of monkeys will leap
to the ridge of her roof, which Hans
has built like a homeland roof,
sound and well-joined, from outlandish wood.
The creatures chatter:
their speech is strange, but no stranger

than what the people spoke whom they met
on the voyage and long journey to come here.
The clearing is still too small;
the jungle's too near, and grows
too fast, in endless rain and
steaming sunlight.
                    Oh,
where can he be? Three days already
have gone since he should have returned.
Oil for the lamp's
getting low . . . but what if right now
with a flashlight, he's making his way
back home? If there's no light,
it will seem like no welcome.

>   *And Hans never comes. Has drowned*
>   *a mile from home, falling*
>   *face forward into a rainswollen stream,*
>   *feet entangled in ropes of vine,*
>   *pack of supplies holding him down.*
>   *Months will pass*
>   *before his bones are discovered.*

Marta rethreads her needle with bluegrey wool.
Her ears ache with listening:
silent slumber of Trudi,
just-audible breathing of Emmi,
unceasing hum and buzz and creaking and rustle
of Amazon forest,
                    thump of her heart.
Posture of waiting,
gesture of darning,
golden halo of lamplight—patient, unknowing,
Marta remains forever
a story without an ending,
broken off in the telling.

Winter Afternoons in the V. & A., pre-W.W.II*

Rain unslanting, unceasing,
darkening afternoon streets.

Within lofty and vast halls,
no one but I, except for

the ancient guards, survivors
of long-ago battles, dozing

under a spell, perched
on the brittle chairs of their sinecure.

My shoes made no sound. I found
everything for myself,

everything in profusion.
Lace of wrought iron,

wrought jewels, Cellini's dreams,
disappearing fore-edge paintings,
chain mail, crinolines, Hokusai, Cotman.
Here was history

as I desired it: magical, specific,
jumbled, unstinting,

a world for the mind to sift
in its hourglass—now, while I was twelve,
or forever.

* See note on page 117.

Heights, Depths, Silence, Unceasing Sound of the Surf

Are they birds or butterflies?
They are sailing, two, not a flock,
more silver-white than the high
clouds, blissful
solitary lovers in infinite azure.

Below them, within the reef,
green shallows, transparent.
                              Beyond,
bounded by angry lace that
flails the coral,
                    the vast,
ironic dark Pacific.

Tonga, 1979

Full moon's sharp
command transforms
the leafspine of each
palmfrond to curved
steel: in absolute
allegiance, uncountable scimitars
hail the unwitnessed hour. The humans
have withdrawn,
curtained,
shuttered.
Stars fall, kamikaze
of ecstasy. The tide
submits and submits.
The moon exacts
penitent joy from lizards,
blood from dreaming women.
Dogs huddle
scared under the frangipani
which lets fall
silently one flower
into the sand.

Tonga, 1979

For Nikolai, Many Thousand Miles Away

The procession that has been crossing
the mountains of your mind since you were six
      and went to Mexico and Grandma showed you
     the trees or clouds moving
                  along the horizon
traverses (clouds for now) this evening the Pacific,
up towards the Equator—horses, men,
centaurs, pilgrims, women with bundles, children;
refugees—or the wild heroes
of a mythology bearing its heavy altars
into the next of its worlds.
               In my hand,
a spiral shell I'd thought
an empty cornucopia
stirs—something looks out of it
and searches my palm with delicate
probing claws, annoyed.
Among the last stains of sundown
the stars return. I look about
for the Southern Cross, and am given—whist!
a shooting star.
         The great world and its wars
are a long way off, news wavers over
the radio and goes out, you and your life
are half a world distant, and in daylight.
                    Here
the surf the reef holds back
speaks without ceasing,
drawing breath
only to utter the next words of its rune.
Crickets begin—deaf to that great insistence—
to praise the night.
Above the dark ocean, over coral, over continents
the riders move, their power
felt but not understood, their will
remote.

'In the field, a
         dark thing.'
'It was, oh, a
         bush or something.'

'No no, a
         dark thing,
something that could
         look at me.'

'Was it like a bear?
         Was it like a moose?'
'No, it was a dark thing
         keeping still to look at me.'

'Was it fierce? Was it foul?
         Was it going to leap upon you?'
'No, it was a shy thing,
         keeping still to look at me.'

Continent

for Dennis Lee

In Canada, a sense
of weight, of burden,
of under the belly of the live
animal land; a clod, or maybe
another beast that clutches
and hangs there. Florida
is its tail, muscular, succulent.

And in the U.S. sometimes
a draft, a current
of air, chills and heightens
the senses, an idea
of mind, of space, of less
dense flesh, something
not ethereal but poignant, a head
crowned with carved ice.

Furry blond wheatfield in
predawn light—I
thought it was a frozen pond.

•

Small town, early morning.
No cars. Sunlit
children wait for the green light.

•

A deer! It leapt the fence,
scared of the train!
Did anyone else see it?

And twenty miles later
again a deer,
the exact same arc of gold!

•

After the trumpets, the
kettledrums, the
bold crescendo of mountains—

prairie subtleties, verbs
declined in gray,
green tones sustained, vast plainsong.

Old People Dozing

Their thoughts are night gulls
following the ferry, gliding
in and out of the window light
and through the reflected wall there, the door
that holds at its center
an arabesque of foam
always at vanishing point,
                            night gulls
that drift on airstream, reverse, swoop
out of sight, return, memory
moving again through the closed door,
white and effortless, hungry.

Sewing together the bits of data
abandoned by the retina.

Well, here was a hand.
We never did see
the lines of its palm.
But fate had inscribed the knuckles,
anyway. Remember?

Oh—that shine,
that reflection on the dark
T.V. screen.
What I was looking at

was a violet,
a shy symbol in purple. No,
a whole jarful of violets.

Their stems are long, they seek
light, perhaps maligned
by imputations of modesty:
nothing cares to be praised by mistake.

                    That shine
of noon on dark glass
distracted me. Plus what I knew.
How briefly
I focussed on pointed petals and
the white sanctum,
the gold herm within,
the magic eyelash-fine stripes of
darker purple
that led to it like strips of prayer rug.

i

Rosalie Gascoigne.

Old nails, their large flat heads
a gray almost silver, bunched
in a blue-glazed stoneware pot—
flowers of the playful mind.
She has fenced one side
of an open invisible square with pickets of feathers—
and here's a bowlful of turret shells,
fingernail size, you can dip your hands in
as into millet, and hear
the music of jostled brittleness.
The room's a temple, the kind that's
thronged with casual, un-awestruck worshippers,
and crowded with small shrines, each
a surprise, and dedicated
each in its turn, to the principle
that nothing is boring, everything's
worth a second look. Presiding,
there's an escutcheon, its emblems
shapes unnamed by geometrists:
slabs of old wood, weathered, residual,
formed by the absence of what was cut
for forgotten purpose, out of their past:
they meet now, austere, graceful,
transfigured by being placed,
being seen.

ii

Memphis Wood.

A studio looped with huge
hanks of wool, of scarlet,

jute and velvet and blue,
rough, braid, swathe, yardage—
textures and colors so profuse, who
can tell noun from adjective,
the process continuous, table, wall,
the woven stitched tied construct
triumphant but never
disowning its origins, scissors
opening roads in landscapes of cloth,
pilgrim needles zigzagging
through gloss and viridian, crimson,
cotton, a motet of fabric, a lace forest
grown by two hands, one vision.

His theme
over and over:

the twang of plucked
catgut
from which struggles
music,

the tufted swampgrass
quicksilvering
dank meadows,

a baby's resolute fury—metaphysic
of appetite and tension.

Not
the bald image, but always—
undulant, elusive, beyond reach
of any dull
staring eye—lodged

among the words, beneath
the skin of image: nerves,

muscles, rivers
of urgent blood, a mind

secret, disciplined, generous and
unfathomable.
                    Over

and over,
his theme
            hid itself and
smilingly reappeared.

                    He loved
persistence—but it must
be linked to invention: landing
backwards, 'facing
into the wind's teeth,'
                    to please him.

He loved
the lotus cup, fragrant
upon the swaying water, loved

the wily mud
pressing swart riches into its roots,

and the long stem of connection.

IV
THE ACOLYTE

Holiday

for K.

i   Postcard

It's not that I can't
get by without you
it's just that
I wasn't lonesome
before I met you.
It's something to do with
salt losing its savor
when that half of the world
one wants to share
stays in one's pocket, half
a crispy delicious bacon sandwich
saved, but for—oh, like Shelley's
posy of dewy flowers, remember,
how he turns to give it—
ah, to whom?

ii   Meeting Again

At Nepenthe, screaming
Steller jays adorn
the gulfs of air. We bask
in sea-sunwarmth. Trees
are blackly green, a phoenix
rages at its prey. I ask
for more coffee and more
of your story. You are telling
of suffering, I suffer
hearing it, but rejoice with you
in the jays' blue, their black
heads, the sheen

63

of feathers and of the sea.
Let's be
best friends: I'll love you
always if you'll love me.

iii   **To Eros**

Eros, O Eros, hail
thy palate, god who knows
good pasta,
good bread,
good Brie.
        The beauty
of freckled squid, flowers of the sea
fresh off the boat, graces
thy altar, Eros, which is in
our eyes. And on our lips
the blood of berries
before we kiss, before we
stumble to bed.
        Our bed
must be, in thy service, earth—
as the strawberry bed
is earth, a ground
for miracles.
        The flesh
is delicate, we must nourish it:
desire hungers
for wine, for clear plain water,
good strong coffee,
as well as for hard cock and
throbbing clitoris and the
glide and thrust of
sentence and paragraph in and up to the
last sweet sigh of a
chapter's ending.

Fragrant with sandalwood, with lightest
oil of almond,

our hearts still flying around and around
                    like silver wheels that
                        can't stop spinning
                            all in a moment,

we lay at rest, holding
tight to each other,
                    not ready yet
to relax and
each move off into separateness.

Then in words
you gave me
to myself:

you made me know I'd
given you what I
wanted to give,
that I hadn't
been travelling alone . . .
                        You wonder
who you are, if you exist, what
you can do with your energy, has it
a center?
            I tell you,
if you can love a woman
the way you love
blackberries,
strawberries in the sun,
the small red onions you plant,
or a hawk riding
the sway of wind over ocean,

if you can make her know it
even for a moment,

you are as real
as earth itself.
              No one confirms
an other unless
he himself rays forth
from a center. This
is the human inscape, this
is the design our fragile
shifting molecules strive to utter
upon the airy spaces where it's
so hard to find foothold.

v   **Postcard**

There's a thistle here
smells of meadowsweet—
so sweet,
so meadow-fragrant
among its prickles.
Yarrow is plentiful,
              that China and old England
              both knew had occult
              power—but I can divine
no messages.
              The roses
have no scent. The sea
here is a landlocked Sound.
It says *I miss you,* breaking
quiet upon the dark sand.

Away he goes, the hour's delightful hero,
arrivederci: and his horse clatters
out of the courtyard, raising
a flurry of straw and scattering hens.

He turns in the saddle waving a plumed hat,
his saddlebags are filled with talismans,
mirrors, parchment histories, gifts and stones,
indecipherable clues to destiny.

He rides off in the dustcloud of his own
story, and when he has vanished she
who had stood firm to wave and watch
from the top step, goes in to the cool

flagstoned kitchen, clears honey and milk and bread
off the table, sweeps from the hearth
ashes of last night's fire, and climbs the stairs
to strip tumbled sheets from her wide bed.

                    Now the long-desired
visit is over. The heroine
is a scribe. Returned to solitude,
eagerly she re-enters the third room,

the room hung with tapestries, scenes that change
whenever she looks away. Here is her lectern,
here her writing desk. She picks a quill,
dips it, begins to write. But not of him.

Mmm, yes, narcissus, mmm.
Licking my scented fingers.
The squat bulb
complacent under its stars.

The Acolyte

The large kitchen is almost dark.
Across the plain of even, diffused light,
copper pans on the wall and the window geranium
tend separate campfires.
Herbs dangle their Spanish moss from rafters.

At the table, floury hands
kneading dough, feet planted
steady on flagstones,
a woman ponders the loaves-to-be.
Yeast and flour, water and salt,
have met in the huge bowl.

It's not
the baked and cooled and cut
bread she's thinking of,
but the way
the dough rises and has a life of its own,

not the oven she's thinking of
but the way
the sour smell changes
to fragrance.

She wants to put
a silver rose or a bell of diamonds
into each loaf;
she wants

to bake a curse into one loaf,
into another, the words that break
evil spells and release
transformed heroes into their selves;
she wants to make
bread that is more than bread.

V
AGE OF TERROR

The Split Mind

A Governor
is signing papers, arranging deals.
His adored grandchild
sits at his feet; he gives her
the architect's model of the nuclear plant to play with.
'A little house' she says,
'with funny fat chimneys.'
'Goddamn commies,' he mutters, crushing
the report on nuclear hazards into a ball and
tossing it across the room, ignoring
the wastebasket and plutonium and the idea
that he could be wrong, one gesture
sufficing for all.
     He strokes
her shining hair. Her death
is in his hands; in hers
the simulacrum of his will to power,
a funerary playhouse. If he lives
to see her change
in the sick radiance later,
after the plant is built,
what will he tell himself?
How deep, how deep
does the split go, the fault line
under the planned facility,
into his mind?

A man and woman
sit by the riverbank.
He fishes,
she reads.
The fish are not biting.
She has not turned the page
for an hour.
The light around them
holds itself taut,
no shadow moves,
but the sky and the woods,
look, are dark.
Night has advanced upon them.

The Vron Woods (North Wales)

In the night's dream of day
the woods were fragrant.
Carapaced, slender, vertical,
      red in the slant
          fragmented light, uprose
Scotch firs,
boughs a vague smoke of
green.
     Underfoot
          the slipping
of tawny needles.

I was wholly there,
aware of each step
in the hum of quietness,
each breath.
       Sunlight
a net
   of discs and lozenges, holding
odor of rosin.

These were the Vron Woods,
       felled
   seven years before I was born,

   levelled,
       to feed a war.

Once a woman went into the woods.
The birds were silent. Why? she said.
Thunder, they told her,
thunder's coming.
She walked on, and the trees were dark
and rustled their leaves. Why? she said.
The great storm, they told her,
the great storm is coming.
She came to the river, it rushed by
without reply, she crossed the bridge,
she began to climb
up to the ridge where grey rocks
bleach themselves, waiting
for crack of doom,
and the hermit
had his hut, the wise man
who had lived since time began.
When she came to the hut
there was no one.
But she heard his axe.
She heard
the listening forest.
She dared not follow the sound
of the axe. Was it
the world-tree he was felling?
Was this the day?

We turn to history looking
for vicious certainties through which
voices edged into song,

engorged fringes of anemone swaying
dreamily through deluge,

gray Lazarus bearing
the exquisite itch and ache of blood returning.

Reason has brought us
more dread than ignorance did.
Into the open
well of centuries

we gaze, and see gleaming,
deep in the black broth at the bottom,
chains of hope by which our forebears
hoisted themselves
hand over hand towards light.

But we
stand at the edge looking back in and knowing
too much to reasonably hope. Their desired light
burns us.

O dread,
drought that dries
the ground of joy till it cracks and
caves in,

O dread,
wind that sweeps up the offal of lies,
sweep my knowledge, too, into oblivion,

drop me back in the well.

No avail.

Each day's terror, almost
a form of boredom—madmen
at the wheel and
stepping on the gas and
the brakes no good—
and each day one,
sometimes two, morning-glories,
faultless, blue, blue sometimes
flecked with magenta, each
lit from within with
the first sunlight.

An English Field in the Nuclear Age

To render it!—*this* moment,
                    haze and halos of
            sunbless'd particulars, knowing
no one,
        not lost and dearest nor
        the unfound,
could,
        though summoned,
        though present,
partake nor proffer vision unless
                    (named, spun, tempered, stain of it
                    sunk into steel of utterance) it
                be wrought:
            (centuries furrowed in oakbole, *this* oak,
            these dogrose pallors, that very company
                    of rooks plodding
                        from stile to stile of the sky):
to render that isolate knowledge, certain
            (shadow of oakleaves, larks
            urging the green wheat into spires)
there is no sharing save in the furnace,
the transubstantiate, acts
                    of passion:
                            (the way

        air, *this* minute, searches
        warm bare shoulders, blind, a lover,

        and how among
        thistles, nettles, subtle silver
        of long-dried cowpads,

        gold mirrors of buttercup satin
        assert eternity as they reflect

nothing, everything, absolute instant,
and dread

holds its breath, for
this minute at least was
not the last).

Grey August

The dog's thigh, the absurd heaven,

the dog's thigh extended, thigh of an Odalisque,
the absurdly pale, shrinking, panic of the sky,
an arched heaven of terror,

like an Etruscan outstretched
to partake of wine the dark
relaxed dog, the heavens intimidated
by smog and preparations for thunder, the sensual patient
placing of himself on the cool linoleum
indoors, outdoors the white sky and humid
thick of air, a veiled twilight, his paws
not twitching, his head at rest,

at last something stirs the
ashleaves to sibilance, an ear
flicks up but disregards
this, the dog has not
seen the sky, he will know
thunder when it comes, if it comes
the heavens will retrieve
their pride, the dog's thigh
quivers, it will be,
for this day,
thunder, not war.

Dedicated to the memory of Karen Silkwood and Eliot Gralla

> '*From too much love of living,*
> > *Hope and desire set free,*
> *Even the weariest river*
> > *Winds somewhere to the sea—*'

But we have only begun
to love the earth.

We have only begun
to imagine the fulness of life.

How could we tire of hope?
—so much is in bud.

How can desire fail?
—we have only begun

to imagine justice and mercy,
only begun to envision

how it might be
to live as siblings with beast and flower,
not as oppressors.

Surely our river
cannot already be hastening
into the sea of nonbeing?

Surely it cannot
drag, in the silt,
all that is innocent?

* See note on page 117.

Not yet, not yet—
there is too much broken
that must be mended,

too much hurt we have done to each other
that cannot yet be forgiven.

We have only begun to know
the power that is in us if we would join
our solitudes in the communion of struggle.

So much is unfolding that must
complete its gesture,

so much is in bud.

Psalm: People Power at the Die-in[*]

Over our scattered tents by night
lightning and thunder called to us.

Fierce rain blessed us,
catholic, all-encompassing.

We walked through blazing morning
into the city of law,

of corrupt order, of invested power.

By day and by night
we sat in the dust,

on the cement pavement we sat down and sang.

In the noon of a long day, sharing the work of the play,
we died together, enacting

the death by which all
shall perish unless we act.

•

Solitaries drew close, releasing
each solitude into its blossoming.

We gave to each other the roses
of our communion—

A culture of gardens, horticulture not agribusiness,
arbors among the lettuce, small terrains.

•

* See note on page 117.

When we tasted the small, ephemeral
harvest of our striving,

great power flowed from us,
luminous, a promise. Yes! . . .

great energy flowed from solitude,
and great power from communion.

About Political Action in Which
Each Individual Acts from the Heart*

When solitaries draw close, releasing
each solitude into its blossoming,

when we give to each other the roses
of our communion—

a culture of gardens, horticulture not agribusiness,
arbors among the lettuce, small terrains—

when we taste in small victories sometimes
the small, ephemeral yet joyful
harvest of our striving,

great power flows from us,
luminous, a promise. Yes! . . . Then

great energy flows from solitude,
and great power from communion.

* See note on page 117.

What It Could Be

Uranium, with which we know
only how to destroy,

lies always under
the most sacred lands—

Australia, Africa, America,
wherever it's found is found an oppressed
ancient people who knew
long before white men found and named it
that there under their feet

under rock, under mountain, deeper
than deepest watersprings, under
the vast deserts familiar
inch by inch to their children

lay a great power.
                    And they knew the folly
of wresting, wrestling, ravaging from the earth
that which it kept
                    so guarded.

Now, now, now at this instant,
men are gouging lumps of that power, that presence,
out of the tortured planet the ancients
say is our mother.
                    Breaking the doors
of her sanctum, tearing the secret
out of her flesh.

But left to lie, its metaphysical weight
might in a million years have proved
benign, its true force being to be
a clue to righteousness—

showing forth
the human power
not to kill, to choose
not to kill: to transcend
the dull force of our weight and will;

that known profound presence, *un*touched,
the sign
providing witness,
                    occasion,
                    ritual
for the continuing act of
*non*violence, of passionate
reverence, active love.

In Memory of Muriel Rukeyser

The last event
of Black Emphasis Week.
In the big auditorium, 2 or 3 Whites, 4 or 5 Blacks,
watch the lynching.

In technicolor,
fictive, not
documentary black and white—

the truth, nonetheless,
white and black.

And the burning.
Familiar—
torching of
brittle timber,
or straw.

        Asia or Alabama,
        the screen gives forth
        an odor. Fat. Hair.
        There will be bones
        in the hot rubble. Black
        bones, or yellow,
        ash white.

The film continues,
reel after reel. Ends. And now
the few who were here—
                scattered, like dim lights
of prairie farms seen from a plane,
              isolate,
                    lost—
have gone out when you turn to leave.

Out, now, into night.
The world is dark, the movie's over,

it's showing again in your head but
your sobs are silent,
you shake

with despair in the
night which holds

trees, soft air,
music pulsing from a dorm,

and a thousand students who chose
not to attend

the truth of fiction,
history, their own. 'No one

to witness and adjust,'

drifting.
   You think: *Perhaps*

we deserve
no more, we humans,
cruel and dull.
No more time.
     We've made
our cathedrals,
had our chance,

blown it.

   You will never
feel more alone than this. Or will you?
Yes. There are 'cliffs of fall'
steeper, deeper.

And you remember
the passion for life, the vision
of love and work

your great intelligent friend had,
who died last week.
Is this despair

a link of those chains she called
the sense of shame?

At Scottsboro she
saw plain,
in black and white,

terror
and hatred;

didn't despair,
grieved, worked,
moved beyond shame,

fought forty years more.

You cross
the darkness

still shaking, enter
the house you've been given,

turn up the desk light,
sit down to plan

the next day. How else
to show your respect?

'No one
to drive the car.' *Well,
let's walk then,* she says,
when you imagine her.

Now. Stop shaking. Imagine her.

She was a cathedral.

A Speech: For Antidraft Rally, D.C., March 22, 1980*

As our planet swings and sways
into its new decade
under the raped moon's weary glance,

I've heard the voices
of high-school kids on the bus home to the projects,
of college students (some of them female, this time)
in the swimmingpool locker room, saying,

'If there's a war—' 'If there's a war—'
'I don't want to get drafted but
if there's a war I'll go'—'If there's a war
I'd like to fight' 'If there's a war
I'll get pregnant'
'Bomb Tehran'—'Bomb Moscow' I heard them say.

Ach! They're the same ones, male and female, who ask,
'Which came first, Vietnam or Korea?'
'What was My Lai?' The same kids who think
Ayatollah Khomeini's a, quote, 'Commie.' Who think
World War Two was fought against, quote, 'Reds,' namely
Hitler and some Japs.

No violence they've seen
on the flickering living-room screen familiar since infancy
or the movies of adolescent dates, the dark
so much fuller of themselves, of each other's presence than of
history (and the history anyway
twisted—not that they have a way to know that)—
     the dark
     vibrant with themselves, with warm breath,
     half suppressed mirth, the wonder

* See note on page 117.

of being alive, terrified, entranced
by sexual fragrance each gives off
among popcorn, clumsy
gestures, the weird
response of laughter when on that screen
death's happening, Wow, *unreal,* and people
suffer, or dream aloud . . . None of that spoon-fed
    violence
prepares them. The disgusting routine horror of war
eludes them. They think
they would die for something they call America,
vague, as true dreams are not; something they call
freedom, the *Free World,* without ever knowing
what *freedom* means, what *torture* means, what *relative*
    means.
They are free to spray walls with crude
assertions—numbers, pathetic names; free
to disco, to disagree—if they're in school—
with the professor. Great. They don't know
that's not enough, they don't know
ass from elbow, blood from ketchup, that knowledge
is kept from them, they've been taught to assume
if there's a war there's
also a future, they know
not only nothing,
in their criminally neglected imaginations, about
the way war always meant
not only dying but killing,
not only killing but seeing
not only your buddy dying but
your buddy in the act of killing, not nice,
not only
your buddy killing but the dying
of those you
killed yourself, not always
quick, and
not always soldiers.

Yes, not only do draft-age people mostly
not know how that kind of war's become almost a pastoral
compared to *new* war, the kind
in which they may find themselves (while the usual
pinkfaced men, smoothshaved, overfed, placed in power
by the parents of those expendable young, continue
to make the decisions they are programmed for) but also

they know nothing at all about radiation
nothing at all about lasers
nothing at all about how the bombs
the Pentagon sits on like some grotesque
chicken caged in its nest and fed
cancerous hormones, exceed and exceed and exceed
Hiroshima, over and over and over, in weight
                              in power
                              in horror
                              of genocide.
                    When they say
'If there's a war,
I'll go,' they don't know
they would be going to kill
                    themselves,
                        their mamas and papas,
                        brothers and sisters
                        lovers.
When they say, 'If there's a war, I'll get pregnant,'
        they don't seem to know
                        that war would destroy that baby.
When they say, 'I'd like to fight,'
                        for quote, 'freedom,'
                        for quote, the 'Free World,'
                        for quote, 'America,'—
for whatever they think they'd be fighting for,
            those children,
                    those children with braces on their teeth,
                        fears in their notebooks,
                        acne on their cheeks,

dreams in their
inarticulate hearts
whom the powerful men at their desks
designate as the age group suitable for registration,
they don't know they'd be fighting
very briefly, very
successfully,
quite conclusively,
for the destruction of this small
lurching planet, this confused
lump of
rock and soil, ocean and air,
on which our songs, cathedrals, gestures
of faith and splendor
have grown like delicate moss, and now
may or may not survive
the heavy footsteps of our inexcusable ignorance,
the chemical sprays of our rapacious idiocy,
our minds that are big enough
to imagine love, imagine peace, imagine
community—but may not
be big enough to learn in time
how to say no.
My dear
fellow-humans, friends, strangers, who would be friends
if there were time—
let us *make* time, let us unite to say
NO to the drift to war, the drift
to take care of little disasters by making a
big disaster and then
the last disaster,
from which
no witness will rise,
no seeds.
Let us unite to tell
all we have learned about old-fashioned war's
vomit and shit, about new fashioned war's
abrupt end to all hope—

unite to tell what we know to the wholebodied young,
unwitting victims lined up ready already
like calves at the pen for slaughter;
share what we know, until no more
young voices talk of 'If there's a war,' but all say
No, and again no to the draft, and no to war,
and no to the sacrifice
of anyone's blood to the corporate beast that dreams
it can always somehow
save its own skin.
                 Let our different dream,
and more than dream, our acts
of constructive refusal generate
struggle. And love. We must dare to win
not wars, but a future
in which to live.

I have a small grain of hope—
one small crystal that gleams
clear colors out of transparency.

I need more.

I break off a fragment
to send you.

Please take
this grain of a grain of hope
so that mine won't shrink.

Please share your fragment
so that yours will grow.

Only so, by division,
will hope increase,

like a clump of irises, which will cease to flower
unless you distribute
the clustered roots, unlikely source—
clumsy and earth-covered—
of grace.

Between the fear
of the horror of Afterwards
and the despair
in the thought of no Afterwards,
we move abraded,
each gesture scraping us
on the millstones.

In dream
there was an Afterwards:
the unknown device—
a silver computer as big as a
block of offices at least,
floating
like Magritte's castle on its rock, aloft
in blue sky—
did explode,
there was
a long moment of cataclysm,
light
of a subdued rose-red suffused
all the air before
a rumbling confused darkness ensued,
but
I came to,
face down,
and found
my young sister alive near me,
and knew my still younger brother
and our mother and father
were close by too,
and, passionately relieved, I
comforted my shocked sister,
still not daring
to raise my head,

only stroking and kissing her arm,
afraid to find devastation around us
though we, all five of us,
seemed to have survived—and I readied myself
to take rollcall: 'Paul Levertoff? Beatrice Levertoff?'

And then in dream—not knowing
if this device, this explosion, were radioactive or not,
but sure that where it had centered
there must be wreck, terror,
fire and dust—
the millstones
commenced their grinding again,

and as in daylight
again we were held between them, cramped,
scraped raw by questions:

perhaps, indeed, we were safe; perhaps
no worse was to follow?—but . . .
what of our gladness, when there,
       where the core of the strange
       roselight had flared up
       out of the detonation of brilliant
       angular silver,
there must be others, others in agony,
and as in waking daylight,
the broken dead?

We live in history, says one.
We're flies on the hide of Leviathan, says another.

Either way, says one,
fears and losses.

And among losses, says another,
the special places our own roads were to lead to.

Our deaths, says one.
That's right, says another,
now it's to be a mass death.

Mass graves, says one, are nothing new.
No, says another, but this time there'll be no graves,
all the dead will lie where they fall.

Except, says one, those that burn to ash.
And are blown in the fiery wind, says another.

How can we live in this fear? says one.
From day to day, says another.

I still want to see, says one,
where my own road's going.

I want to live, says another, but where can I live
if the world is gone?

Writing in the Dark

It's not difficult.
Anyway, it's necessary.

Wait till morning, and you'll forget.
And who knows if morning will come.

Fumble for the light, and you'll be
stark awake, but the vision
will be fading, slipping
out of reach.

You must have paper at hand,
a felt-tip pen—ballpoints don't always flow,
pencil points tend to break. There's nothing
shameful in that much prudence: those are your tools.

Never mind about crossing your t's, dotting your i's—
but take care not to cover
one word with the next. Practice will reveal
how one hand instinctively comes to the aid of the other
to keep each line
clear of the next.

Keep writing in the dark:
a record of the night, or
words that pulled you from depths of unknowing,
words that flew through your mind, strange birds
crying their urgency with human voices,

or opened
as flowers of a tree that blooms
only once in a lifetime:

words that may have the power
to make the sun rise again.

We were trying to put the roots back,
wild and erratic straying root-limbs,
trying to fit them into the hole that was
cleancut in clay, deep but not
wide enough; or wide but too square—trying
to get the roots back into earth
before they dried out and died.
Ineptly we pulled and pushed
striving to encompass so many rivers
of wood and fiber in one confinement without
snapping the arteries of sap, the force
of life springing in them that made them
spring away from our hands—
we knew our own life was
tied to that strength, that strength we knew would
ebb away if we could not find within us
the blessed guile to tempt
its energy back into earth,
into the quiet depths from which we had
rashly torn it, and now clumsily
struggled to thrust it back not into sinuous corridors
fit for its subtleties, but obstinately
into an excavation dug by machine.
                    And I wake,
as if from dream, but discover
even this digging, better than nothing,
has not yet begun.

Unresolved

'See the blood in the streets'
Neruda

i

Fossil shells, far inland; a god; bones;
they lie exposed by the backhoe.

Little stars continue to confide their silken hopes
among rough leaves.

In blood, his own, a man writes on a wall,
Revolution or Death. Not then. Now.

Now in a dry crevice, the corn, His Grace
the God of Maíz,
wraps his parchment about the green nub
destined to be gold.

ii

When one has begun to believe
the grip of doubt tightens.

A child is born. Earthquake kills
20,000. That's the commonplace.

A dialectic always half perceived. We know
no synthesis.

iii

What we fear begins and begins. Fools and criminals
rule the world. Life is a handful of stones
loosely held in their fists.

iv

Merciful earthquake! Majestic lava pouring
unstinted from mountain's fire! Ceremonious flood!
You ravage but are not hideous. Compare:

chopped-off heads stare in El Salvador
at their steaming torsos, flat circles
                        that were their necks revealing
closepacked flesh and bone and the sectioned tubes
                        through which
food and drink used to pass, and breath. See it on film.

Run the scene over again. And over again.
For verisimilitude, many hundred times
will not be enough.
                        Just out of range—
of the camera, not of the bullets—
babies, tossed high for the Junta's
target practice, plummet
past their parents' upturned screaming faces and hit
the reddening river with small splashes.
Hear it. It sounds like someone idly pitching rocks;
as if a terrified dog were being stoned
while it swam in circles; while it drowned.

v

We know so much of daily bread,
of every thread of lovingly knit compassion;

garments of love clothe us, we rest
our heads upon darkness; when we wake

sapphire transparency calls forth our song.
And this is the very world, the same, the world

of vicious power, of massacre.
Our song is a bird that wants
to sing as it flies, to be
the wings of praise, but doubt

binds tight its wire to hold down
flightbones, choke back breath.
We know no synthesis.

With my brother I ran
willingly into the sea:

our mother, our sister too,
all of us free and naked.

We knew nothing of risk,
only the sacred pleasure

of sun and sand and the
beckoning ocean:

in, into the leaping
green of the lilt of it.

But at once a vast wave
unfurled itself to seize me, furled

about me, bore me as a bubble
back and tilted aslant from

all shore; all sight, sound, thought of others swept
instantly into

remote distance—
                    Now is wholly
this lucent rampart up which

I can't climb but where
I cling, powerless, unable

to distinguish terror from delight, calm
only in the one wanhope, to keep

a breath alive above the enormous
roar of the sunlaughing utter

force of the great wave, ride
on in its dangerous cradle of swift
transparent silks that curve
in steel over and round me, bearing

westward, outward, beyond
all shores, the great

wave still mounting, moving,
poised and poised in its

flood of emerald, dark unshatterable
crystal of its

unfathomed purpose—

Mass for the Day of St. Thomas Didymus

i Kyrie
ii Gloria
iii Credo
iv Sanctus
v Benedictus
vi Agnus Dei

i   Kyrie

O deep unknown, guttering candle,
beloved nugget lodged
in the obscure heart's
last recess,
have mercy upon us.

We choose from the past, tearing morsels to feed
pride or grievance.
We live in terror
of what we know:

death, death, and the world's
death we imagine
        and cannot imagine,
we who may be
the first and the last witness.

We live in terror
of what we do not know, .
in terror of not knowing,
of the limitless, through which freefalling
forever, our dread
sinks and sinks,
                or
        of the violent closure of all.

Yet our hope lies
in the unknown,
in our unknowing.

O deep, remote unknown,
O deep unknown,
Have mercy upon us.

ii   **Gloria**

Praise the wet snow
       falling early.
Praise the shadow
       my neighbor's chimney casts on the tile roof
even this gray October day that should, they say,
have been golden.
             Praise
the invisible sun burning beyond
    the white cold sky, giving us
light and the chimney's shadow.
Praise
god or the gods, the unknown,
that which imagined us, which stays
our hand,
our murderous hand,
              and gives us
still,
in the shadow of death,
       our daily life,
       and the dream still
of goodwill, of peace on earth.
Praise
flow and change, night and
the pulse of day.

iii   Credo

I believe the earth
exists, and
in each minim mote
of its dust the holy
glow of thy candle.
Thou
unknown I know,
thou spirit,
giver,
lover of making, of the
wrought letter,
wrought flower,
iron, deed, dream.
Dust of the earth,
help thou my
unbelief. Drift,
gray become gold, in the beam of
vision. I believe and
interrupt my belief with
doubt. I doubt and
interrupt my doubt with belief. Be,
belovéd, threatened world.
              Each minim
mote.
          Not the poisonous
luminescence forced
out of its privacy,
the sacred lock of its cell
broken. No,
the ordinary glow
of common dust in ancient sunlight.
Be, that I may believe. Amen.

iv   **Sanctus**

Powers and principalities—all the gods,
angels and demigods, eloquent animals, oracles,
storms of blessing and wrath—

> all that Imagination
> has wrought, has rendered,
> striving, in throes of epiphany—

> naming, forming—to give
> to the Vast Loneliness
> a hearth, a locus—

send forth their song towards
the harboring silence, uttering
the ecstasy of their names, the multiform
name of the Other, the known
Unknown, unknowable:

sanctus, hosanna, sanctus.

v   **Benedictus**

Blesséd is that which comes in the name of the spirit,
that which bears
the spirit within it.

The name of the spirit is written
in woodgrain, windripple, crystal,

in crystals of snow, in petal, leaf,
moss and moon, fossil and feather,

blood, bone, song, silence,
very word of
very word,

flesh and
vision.

> (But what of the deft infliction
> upon the earth, upon the innocent,
> of hell by human hands?
>
> Is the word
> audible under or over the gross
> cacophony of malevolence?
> Yet to be felt
>> on the palm, in the breast,
> by deafmute dreamers,
>> a vibration
>> known in the fibers of
>> the tree of nerves, or witnessed
>> by the third eye to which
>> sight and sound are one?
>
> What of the emptiness,
> the destructive vortex that whirls
> no word with it?)

In the lion's indolence,
    there spirit is,
in the tiger's fierceness
    that does not provide in advance
but springs
                only as hunger prompts,
                and the hunger
                of its young.

Blesséd is that which utters
its being,
the stone of stone,
the straw of straw,
                for there

spirit is.
But can the name
utter itself
in the downspin of time?
Can it enter
the void?
Blesséd
be the dust. From dust the world
utters itself. We have no other
hope, no knowledge.
The word
chose to become
flesh. In the blur of flesh
we bow, baffled.

vi   **Agnus Dei**

Given that lambs
are infant sheep, that sheep
are afraid and foolish, and lack
the means of self-protection, having
neither rage nor claws,
venom nor cunning,
what then
is this 'Lamb of God'?

This pretty creature, vigorous
to nuzzle at milky dugs,
woolbearer, bleater,
leaper in air for delight of being, who finds in astonishment
four legs to land on, the grass
all it knows of the world?
With whom we would like to play,
whom we'd lead with ribbons, but may not bring
into our houses because
it would soil the floor with its droppings?

What terror lies concealed
in strangest words, *O lamb*
of God that taketh away
the Sins of the World: an innocence
    smelling of ignorance,
    born in bloody snowdrifts,
    licked by forebearing
dogs more intelligent than its entire flock put together?

        God then,
    encompassing all things, is
    defenseless? Omnipotence
    has been tossed away, reduced
    to a wisp of damp wool?

        And we,
    frightened, bored, wanting
only to sleep till catastrophe
has raged, clashed, seethed and gone by without us,
    wanting then
to awaken in quietude without remembrance of agony,

     we who in shamefaced private hope
    had looked to be plucked from fire and given
    a bliss we deserved for having imagined it,

    is it implied that *we*
    must protect this perversely weak
    animal, whose muzzle's nudgings
    suppose there is milk to be found in us?
    Must hold to our icy hearts
    a shivering God?

       •

So be it.

      Come, rag of pungent
      quiverings,

            dim star.

                 Let's try
          if something human still
          can shield you,

                 spark
          of remote light.

What I must not forget
is the world of the white herons

complete to the last hair of pondweed,
a world the size of an apple,

perfect and undefiled, with its own sky, its air,
flora and fauna, distance, mysteries.

What I must not forget
is the knowledge that vision gave me

that it was not a fragile, only, other world,
there were, there are (I learned) a host,

each unique, yet each having
the grace of recapitulating

a single radiance, multiform.

This is what, remembering,
I must try, telling myself again,

to tell you. For that the vision
was given me: to know and share,

passing from hand to hand, although
its clarity dwindles in our confusion,

the amulet of mercy.

Notes

13 'The Dragon-Fly Mother.' Readers may be interested to read 'The Earthwoman and the Waterwoman' (*Collected Earlier Poems*, p. 31), a poem written in 1957, to which this 1979 poem makes some allusions.

48 'Winter Afternoons in the V. & A., pre-W. W. II.' For those unfamiliar with London: the V. & A. is the Victoria and Albert Museum in South Kensington. Nowadays it is crowded with visitors.

82 'Beginners.' The opening stanza is Swinburne, slightly misquoted because I had remembered it this way for many years.

84 'Psalm: People Power . . .' and 'About Political Action . . .' The
86 long version derives directly from events described in prose as 'With the Seabrook Natural Guard in Washington, 1978' (*Light Up the Cave*, p. 162). The short version, detached from that particular occasion, is an alternative rather than a substitute.

92 'A Speech . . .' Written for an antidraft rally (which was attended by 35,000) this piece really *is* a speech, and not properly classifiable as a poem. I decided to include it because it is not prose either, and because many people—draft counsellors and high-school teachers especially—have requested me to make it generally available.

117

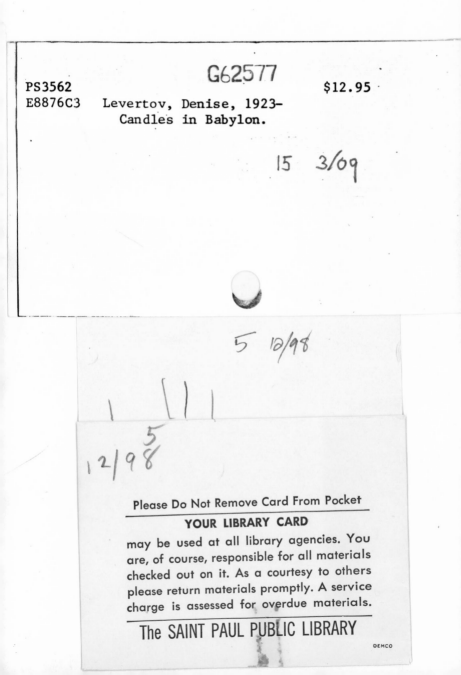